Distracted

Finding God in a Chaotic World

Sherman Burkhead

Renown Publishing

Distracted / Sherman Burkhead
ISBN: 978-1-945793-85-1

This book is dedicated to my very best friend and wife, Kim. You are my greatest supporter and you have willingly followed me as I have pursued God's call upon my life. You are truly a gift from our gracious Lord.

CONTENTS

A Time Thief

The demands begin before your feet even hit the floor in the morning. Your alarm jolts you awake. Your children (or dog, cat, hamster, parrot, etc.) begin to voice their needs. You are hungry, sleepy, and stiff as you stumble into the kitchen for a cup of coffee. You think to yourself, *"I really should stop and pray."* But then all the things you need to do before you leave the house fill your mind and you promise yourself, *"I'll pray later."* Then your to-do list explodes, and the race is on.

And after a busy day, you find the same scene playing in reverse, with all the things that need to be done before you go to bed demanding your attention. As you drift off to sleep, worn out from the demands of the day, you promise to do better and think, *"Tomorrow I will begin my day in prayer."* Then the cycle begins all over again.

It's not that you intend for things to be this way. There is simply so much to do and so many urgent things calling out to you. Your loved ones deserve your full attention and they look to you and depend on you. Your work is important; it is what puts food on the table and braces in your kids' mouths. Being responsible is a necessary part of life; just think of the alternative. These things, and many others, are a priority.

But have you prioritized the thing that breathes life into all other aspects of your day? Do you spend time meditating on God's life-giving Word every day? Do you find time to be alone with God, pouring your heart out to Him, growing your relationship with Him? Are you regularly seeking His council and His guidance? Are you daily praising Him for His goodness?

A lot of things you do, even good things, are distracting you from what truly matters. A lot of what happens to you during the day distracts you as well. If we are honest, a lot of unnecessary things are a distraction. To make it even more difficult, a lot of what distracts you doesn't seem like a distraction at all.

So how do you discern what is a necessary priority or an unwelcome deterrent? How do you prioritize all these important things that you need to accomplish to maximize your effectiveness in your daily life and still be rooted in the One who gives you the grace to do it all?

The truth is, our tendency to be distracted exacts a terrible price because it robs time from the things you value and spends it on the trivial. Do you ever wonder what happened to your day? Your week? Your month? Do you ever wonder if you missed something important—especially in relationships—because you're just trying to keep your head above water? This is especially true in your relationship with God.

God is always waiting for you to come and spend alone

time with Him. But you are living in a crazy, busy world surrounded by a gazillion things, important and trivial, demanding your attention. And He, the One who gave you life and sustains your existence, waits.

Doesn't that seem like your priorities are wrong? The most important and powerful Being in the universe wants to spend time with you, but you are just too busy. That isn't the way you want it to be, and you instinctively know it. However, you're caught in a rut and don't know how to get out.

There is no way for this book to rescue you from the 21st century, but it can help you find time and space for God, the One in whom "we live and move and have our being" (Acts 17:28). He is the One who not only crafted you and gave you life, but came to the earth to rescue you. In this book we will:

- Explore the allure of good things that distract us from the best things.

- Look at how to put fear in its place because fear is a huge distraction.

- Unpack some wrong assumptions leading to a distracted, unfocused life.

- Examine your priorities to support what you were created for: knowing and following Jesus.

- Develop some practical habits to help you grow past the things that distract you and help you grow in deeper fellowship with God, as well as in your spiritual maturity.

At the end of each chapter, workbook sections will provide questions, journal prompts, and action steps that give you practical tools to focus your life fully on deepening your relationship with God.

The Westminster Shorter catechism says, rightly, "The chief end of man is to glorify God and enjoy him forever."[1]

Let me help you commit to this high and holy calling. Let me help you set aside the distractions, the fears, and the idols that clamor for your allegiance, and realign your life back on God.

WORKBOOK

Introduction Questions

Journal Prompt: Describe a time when you lost an opportunity or missed something important because of distraction.

Then make a list that describes:

- Demands in your life that pull your focus away from God

- Distractions with your time that pull your priorities away from God

- Delights of the world that pull your joy from God

Are these things keeping you from glorifying God and enjoying Him? Could a changed mindset help you to glorify God through distractions instead of letting them pull you from Him? Ask God to speak to your heart and commit to obey His leading as you read through the rest of this book.

Introduction Notes

_____

_____

_____

_____

_____

_____

_____

_____

_____

_____

_____

_____

_____

_____

_____

_____

_____

_____

_____

_____

_____

CHAPTER ONE

Driven to Distraction

Be still, and know that I am God; I will be exalted among the nations, I will be exalted in the earth!
                                                    —*Psalm 46:10*

Missionary and preacher Paul Washer once said, "One of the greatest attacks of the enemy is to make you busy."[2] I believe this is the truth. If you fill your life with activities, hobbies, interests, worries, gadgets, and random goals—and add to that the American ideal of multitasking—you will live in a continual state of exhaustion!

It's mind-boggling. When you're at home, you're thinking about work or school or about paying the bills or what's for dinner. When you're at work, where you're supposed to do the things you're getting paid for, your mind is often elsewhere. You worry about the leaky roof or fantasy football or the latest news. Then that little device in your pocket buzzes and beeps to tell you that you have emails, text messages, voicemails, and phone calls.

Created for Connection

Technology was supposed to make us more productive and connected; it was meant to buy us more flextime. In reality, however, technology separates and rules us. You spend time checking your phone repeatedly from the first thing in the morning to the last thing at night. Even your family time is sullied. You can sit together for hours on end without even saying a word to each other.

Commuting to work or driving to run errands used to be a good time to pray or talk to others riding with you. Now everyone else in the car is captivated by their devices. Even drivers have a hard time letting go of their phones on the road. Admit it—you've answered the phone while you're driving, and I'm not talking about your hands-free option. If we are really honest, many of us have checked text messages and our social media feed while driving.

What happens when you get a call or a text message while you're trying to pray? Do you answer the phone? Do you check it to see if it is someone important enough to interrupt your time with God? John McArthur once wrote:

> The more you focus on yourself, the more distracted you will be from the proper path. The more you know Him and commune with Him, the more the Spirit will make you like Him. And the more you're like Him, the better you will understand His utter sufficiency for all life's difficulties. And that is the only way to know *real* satisfaction.[3]

Your relationship with God is the most important relationship in your life. This fact cannot be overstated. Your relationship with God is more important than that with your grandma, your spouse, or your children. God is the most important person in the universe. You were created to live in an intimate relationship with Him.

It has been said that there's a God-shaped hole in your heart and nothing in the world but God is going to fill it. Now the Bible doesn't say anything about a hole in our heart, but the image does help us to understand that nothing in this world can give you the joy and satisfaction that you need apart from Him.[4]

Nothing and no one else will meet your deepest need: not money, not fame, not a successful career, not relationships, not your son being drafted in the first round of the MLB, not sex, not even religion. Without God your life will be needy, broken, and vain because you were created by Him to be connected to Him.

So why do we struggle so hard to stay connected to Him? It's not that you don't have time for God. Rather, you're too distracted with other things and you are letting them get in the way of that connection. You are prioritizing other things over your relationship with God.

I have heard so many people say to me, "I don't have time to read the Bible. I don't have time to be pray. I don't have time for discipleship. I am just too busy with work, or with the kids or ____"—you fill in the blank. Let me tell you plainly: you don't have enough time *not* to spend time with God! Martin Luther once said, "I have so much to do that I shall spend the first three hours in prayer."[5] He understood where his strength came from, and you would do well to recognize the same thing.

Before you trusted in Christ, your sin separated you

from God and you couldn't have had a relationship with Him even if you had wanted to. Then you heard the good news: Christ died in your place, took away your sin, and gave you His righteousness so you could be close to God. Christ literally tore down the barrier between you and the Father. Through repentance and faith in Jesus, you can now have a fruitful, life-giving relationship with God. This is the relationship that you were created for.

The context of Psalm 46 suggests that this psalm was written during a time of war and turbulence. That makes verse 10, quoted at the beginning of this chapter, even more profound—because the circumstances were certainly not favorable for "being still" in the presence of the Lord. Obviously, connecting with God and maintaining a healthy relationship with Him was a major priority for the psalmist and the same ought to be true for us.

The Consequences of Disconnection

Even though God has provided you with a direct connection to Him, it is possible that you don't maintain an up-close, personal relationship with God. You may live an up-and-down, chaotic life full of the many distractions we have considered—and more. Let's face it; there are thousands of things competing for your attention. Any of those things can get in the way of your relationship with God.

When you get disconnected from God, even as a believer, you experience several negative consequences as a result. First you lose sight of Christ and the gospel. I don't know about you, but I can't afford to lose sight of the gospel. I know that I'm a broken sinner, prone to making mistakes and wandering away from God. The gospel reminds me that I'm loved by God, not because of what I do for Him, but because of what Jesus has done for me.

Paul told us, "For by grace you have been saved through faith. And this is not your own doing; it is the gift of God" (Ephesians 2:8). I need to keep reminding myself of this over and over, and so do you.

If you lose sight of this truth, you'll begin to think that God's love for you must be earned by your works. It delights Satan if he can convince you this is true. Then you become legalistic and make a lot of rules about what you must do to make God love you. Alternately, you may become fatalistic. Constantly aware of your shortcomings, you think, *"What's the point? I'm never going to be good enough. I might as well live in sin."*

Neglecting your relationship with God can also cause you to start trying to live your life on your own strength. This includes trying to solve all of your own problems and to make your own decisions as a declaration of independence from God. You still believe in Him but forget that God is there for and with you. You try to fix things and handle your problems in your own strength, fail miserably, and then you remember that you didn't even take the time to pray about the situation!

How many times have you made a decision that affects your life and you never even thought to stop and pray about it? No wonder things didn't work out! James 1:5 encourages us to ask God for wisdom. Clearly, God never intended for you to try to figure out everything on your own. Instead, "Trust in the LORD with all your heart, and do not lean on your own understanding" (Proverbs 3:5).

Because you are in a relationship with God, you have been given access to all the power—every bit of it—all the answers and help for every conceivable situation you will ever face. But when you get distracted from God, you begin to live as if He's not there.

Therefore, as 1 Peter 5:8 admonishes:

> *Be sober-minded, be watchful. Your adversary the devil prowls around like a roaring lion, seeking someone to devour.*

Neglecting your relationship with God can make you more susceptible to temptation. Sin and temptation are always around the corner. You are continually being hunted by your enemy. The devil is a cunning adversary looking for a way to bring you down. When your relationship with God is distant, you isolate yourself from His protection. It makes you easy prey.

You also miss opportunities and blessings that only are found in His presence—blessings like true joy and a peace that "surpasses all understanding" (Philippians 4:7). You will experience more fear, worry, and anxiety and less peace, joy, and comfort when you are disconnected from God. When I talk to people about their struggles, I always ask them the same question: "How's your time with God?" Invariably, those who experience the most fear, worry, and anxiety are the ones who have been trapped by the distractions around them, rather than regularly seeking the face of God.

Make and Keep an Appointment with God

The foundation for this book, the key to overcoming the distractions in your life, is making and keeping an appointment with God. I know this might sound overly simple but it is the truth.

Set a time and place to spend time alone with God every single day. If you haven't already set that time then you need to do it today. Right now. In fact take out your calendar or your digital device and schedule some uninterrupted, daily, quiet time for you to be alone with the Creator of the universe. Do it now. Pick a time and a place before you read the next paragraph. God has top priority. And the good news is you don't even need to work around His schedule! The Lord graciously meets with you whenever you call out to Him.

Once you have a time and a place set aside, the important thing is to keep your appointment with God. It's that important and that simple. Only time spent with Him will help you grow in your knowledge of Him. Again I know this might seem simplistic, but it is the truth. Time in prayer, reading the Word, meditating on God's Word, and worshiping Him—these are all means that God uses to grow your relationship and draw you closer to Him.

Now before you protest and point out how busy you are, just remember if anyone had a busy and hectic life, it was Jesus Himself. There were always people clamoring for His attention, needing to be healed and wanting to see Him, talk to Him, and be with Him. He was busy from sunup to sundown and beyond. At times, Jesus was so busy that He didn't even eat, prompting his own family to think He was crazy (Mark 3:20–21). Yet while Jesus was on earth, He made it a priority to find a place, set aside some time, and spend it alone with the Father. Jesus needed that time. If it was important to Jesus, the Son of God, it's important for us too. And if He could find time, so can you.

Here are some practical tips for ensuring you get the most out of your time spent with God:

Turn off your cell phone! A cell phone has the capacity to be an ever-present distraction. Turn it off and tuck it away in a drawer for the sake of preserving your time with God. It might make you feel uneasy to turn it off. That's okay. Do it anyway.

Read His Word every day. If you want to make God the supreme love of your life, you must be in a position to hear Him through His Word. You might say you don't have time, but I don't believe it! We can always make time for something that matters to us. I make excuses too, and I understand how busy you are, but I know there's probably some social media or TV time you could give up. You can start by committing to spend five or ten minutes reading the Word and build from there as your appetite grows.

If you're not a reader, then download a Bible app and listen to the Bible in any version you want. Listen while you drive to work, do the dishes, go for a walk, or exercise at the gym. There is always a way to make time for God's Word in your life.

Study the Bible. Research for yourself what God says about anything you need wisdom for or are curious about. Studying the Bible goes beyond merely reading it. Reading the Bible is absolutely vital to your relationship with

God, but so is studying the Bible. Bible study is where you slow down and really dive into the text, focusing, concentrating, observing, and encountering what God is saying. Every word of the Bible is the very Word of God (2 Timothy 3:16) and is worthy of in-depth exploration.

Now before you feel intimidated, understand that studying the Bible can be done in many different ways. You could do a word study, where you choose a word and look at all the places and ways it is used in the Bible. You can even look into the different Hebrew and Greek meanings of the words. There are a lot of great online tools like blueletterbible.org or biblehub.com to help.

You could also choose a book of the Bible to study and read a reputable commentary to deepen your understanding of the context and meaning of a text. I personally like the *Christ-Centered Exposition* commentary series produced by Holman, John MacArthur's Bible commentaries, Warren Wiersbe's Bible commentaries, and the *Expositor's Bible Commentary* series by Zondervan. You can also read books that help you study God's Word more in depth. R.C. Sproul's *Knowing Scripture*, John MacArthur's *How to Get the Most out of God's Word*, and Duvall and Hayes' *Grasping God's Word* are great resources.

It may sound overwhelming, but remember that you can start small. Maybe just once a week, spend some time intentionally digging deeper into Scripture. Grab your Bible, a note pad, and a pen and begin writing down what you see in the text. You may even look into signing up for a Bible study group at church that will help you learn how to go deeper into the Word of God.

Meditate on the Word of God. This means that God's Word is always on your mind—that's how it permeates your heart. When you're reading or studying the Bible or listening to a sermon, many times a verse will stand out to you. Write the verse down on a little card, put it on your mirror or your dashboard or by your phone charger—somewhere you're going to look—and read it. As you go through the day, think about it. That's meditating—you don't have to have scented candles and a dark room. It's the simple act of intentionally thinking about God's Word.

Do what the Word says. James wrote, "be doers of the word, and not hearers only" (James 1:22). If you want your mind to be changed and focused on Christ, you need to do what Jesus tells you to do: love God with all your heart and love your neighbor as yourself (Matthew 22:37–39). Love your enemies. Seek first the kingdom of God and His righteousness (Matthew 6:33). Trust God and lean not on your own understanding (Proverbs 3:5). Pick up your cross daily and follow Jesus (Luke 9:23).

If you love Him, you will keep His commandments (John 14:15). It's that simple. Spend time with God, learn from His Word, and allow it to transform how you live your life.

Talk to God. This is another way of saying pray. This is your opportunity to speak to the God who created you. Put down your to-do list, even put down your Bible, and open up and share your heart with God. He wants to hear from you. Peter encouraged believers to "[cast] all your anxieties on him, because he cares for you" (1 Peter 5:7). Paul says, "do not be anxious about anything, but in everything by prayer and supplication with thanksgiving let your requests be made known to God" (Philippians 4:6). God has given you the privilege to talk with him anytime you want. Take Him up on it.

Worship God. Whether through song or prayers of gratefulness, worship is a great way to remind yourself of the goodness of God. You can sing along to worship songs that are focused on God's goodness and His awesome power or even choose a praise-filled psalm and sing it to your own tune. If you are not musically inclined, you can worship God with prayers of thankfulness. Praise God with your prayers that acknowledge who He is and all He has done. Worship is a great way to pursue that connection with God and to fill your mind and heart with peace.

I realize that there is more to worship than singing and praying. Worship can be preaching, listening to the Word being preached, doing a job to the best of your ability, and loving your neighbor. All those things are worship and are good and important. However, for this application, I am writing about the value of singing and praying to God.

Preach the gospel to yourself. Remind yourself all the time who you are in Christ: a child of God. Life is always, always, always about the gospel. It is the central truth you must hold onto, think about, talk about, meditate on, and sing about all the time. The gospel overcomes your fears and weaknesses.

Remember all that Jesus has done for you! You were dead in your sins with no hope to save yourself. If that hadn't changed, you would spend all eternity in torment, cast into hell. But the good news is that God the Father sent God the Son to the earth to live the life you couldn't live, fulfill the law you couldn't fulfill, and He willingly went to the cross and was tortured. He endured the full wrath of almighty God that you deserved and He died in your place.

On the cross, He took away all your sins, washed away all your iniquities, and gave you His righteousness so that you can stand before God unashamed. It's no longer your sin God sees; it's the righteousness of Christ (2 Corinthians 5:21).

But that is not the end of the story. Three days later, Christ rose from the dead, proving that the debt was paid and that He is who He claimed to be, God in the flesh. He proved that He can do what He promised to do—save you from your sin. And then, forty days later, Jesus ascended into heaven where He sits at the right hand of the Father, interceding for you at this very moment.

Jesus sent God the Holy Spirit to come and live inside of those who believe in Him. Because of Christ's finished work on the cross, you now can spend all eternity in heaven in the presence of God. All you need to do is repent of your sins, put your trust in Christ (Mark 1:15), confess that Jesus is Lord, and believe in your heart that God raised Him from the dead, and you will be saved (Romans 10:9–10).

Plug in and stay plugged into God's family at a local church. Whatever you might say, the Bible says nothing about "lone ranger" Christians. They don't exist. You will not grow to spiritual maturity, become the person God is calling you to be, or make Him the supreme love of your life on your own. It just won't happen.

You were created to be part of a family, a church, part of His body—not just the universal body, but the local body as well. Paul said, "Let us consider how to stir one another up for love and good works, not neglecting to meet together as is the habit of some, but encouraging one another, and all the more as you see the Day drawing near" (Hebrews 10:24–25).

The fact is every believer is called to be an active part of a local church. If you are not part of a church, make it your priority this week to find a strong, Christ-centered, Biblical church and get plugged in. You and your family need the fellowship and the leadership of a pastor who has been called by God to shepherd your souls.

It may take you time to find your rhythm as you re-prioritize your life and make God your ultimate focus. However, as you intentionally choose to make and keep an appointment with God, your relationship with Him will continue to grow naturally. It is on this foundation that everything else in this book is built upon.

I hope that after reading this chapter you are convinced that you need to understand how and when you are distracted from God and how to avoid the predicament by making and keeping a daily appointment with God.

WORKBOOK

Chapter One Questions

Question: Would you describe yourself as a busy person? Why or why not? Are there things you could cut back on or eliminate from your schedule to allow yourself to live a more intentional life?

Question: Recall your salvation testimony when you believed the gospel and entered into a relationship with Christ. What time in your life did you feel the most closely connected to Him? If you do not have that same nearness in your walk with Him now, what changed? What steps can you take to walk in that closeness with God again?

_____

_____

_____

_____

_____

_____

_____

_____

_____

_____

_____

Question: What are evidences of living life dependent upon God's wisdom, direction, and strength? What are evidences of trying to do it all—including obeying Christ—in your own power? Which list more accurately describes you at this moment?

Journal: Think about your average day and identify regular patterns of distraction. In a journal or notebook, write down the unchanging parts of your days (work, eating, sleeping, etc.) as well as your usual free time activities and your typical distractions. Begin praying about God's priorities for your time and how you should spend it. Update your list daily with how you spend your time and review it weekly to see how you are learning to make better choices.

Action: Decide on a time every day that will be devoted to intentionally spending time with God. Keep your appointment! Not only is it an integral part of removing distractions from your life, it's also the very foundation of your relationship with God. As you are making or renewing a commitment to spend time with God every day, take a week-long technology fast. Depending on your career, this may be just a break from social media, online news, etc., but try to arrange a week when you can totally unplug. Start with a day at a time if a week is unrealistic. Evaluate: How is technology impacting your distraction level? In what ways, good or bad, is it impacting your relationship with God?

Chapter One Notes

CHAPTER TWO

The Better Thing

Now as they went on their way, Jesus entered a village. And a woman named Martha welcomed him into her house. And she had a sister called Mary, who sat at the Lord's feet and listened to his teaching. But Martha was distracted with much serving. And she went up to him and said, "Lord, do you not care that my sister has left me to serve alone? Tell her then to help me." But the Lord answered her, "Martha, Martha, you are anxious and troubled about many things, but one thing is necessary. Mary has chosen the good portion, which will not be taken away from her."

—Luke 10:38–42

It might surprise you, but good things can be distractions from the best things. That's what we learn from the story of Martha and Mary. Now Martha, Mary, and Lazarus weren't just followers of Jesus, they were close personal friends. Jesus made a point of coming to see them when He was in town, and they made their home a comfortable place for Him to get some rest and teach His disciples away from the crowds.

In first-century Jewish culture, you were expected to provide a big meal for your guests. When Jesus arrived, Martha was slaving away in the kitchen, but she noticed that her sister Mary was in the next room with Jesus and His disciples. There was so much to be done and Mary wasn't helping! I'm sure you can identify with the situation. Martha was irritated.

It is important to recognize that the fact that Martha was cooking a meal was a good thing; she was honoring Jesus by serving Him to the best of her abilities. It was a loving thing to do. It was a customary thing to do. She sincerely thought it was the best thing to do in that moment, and she believed her sister should have been helping her.

Martha knew Jesus well, so she brought Him her complaint: Mary was just being lazy. But Jesus, rather than just sympathizing with her, helped Martha see the bigger, more important picture. Martha was so distracted by what she thought was a priority that she overlooked the fact that the Son of God was staying at her house! The Messiah was in her living room! His presence and His teaching trumped any big meal. Mary had figured it out and she used the opportunity to sit at His feet and give Him her full attention and love.

You can be so busy serving the Lord that you neglect the Lord Himself. That is a sentence you should highlight or underline. You can be so busy doing something good, like serving the living God, that you neglect time with the Lord himself. That was Martha's issue.

Preparing a meal is important. Eating is also important, but it is short-lived. If you eat food today, you will be hungry again tomorrow. Mary, on the other hand, sat at Jesus' feet feeding her soul, which lasts forever. It's simply a matter of priorities. What is the best, good thing to do?

Both women had a choice to make: to sit and spend time with Jesus or to get busy doing something else. As a Christian, this is a choice you will often need to make as well. Will you be so busy doing all the important, good things that you neglect the most important thing? Or will you make it a point to prioritize time for the *best* good thing?

Potential Distractions

You need to work to provide for your family. It is not God's plan for people to be idle. Work is good and gives you purpose. In fact, work came before the fall of man, so it is very good. But you can give work too much priority. As a recovering workaholic, I'm an expert on this subject!

Recently, I found myself hustling to get to the office earlier and earlier to get things done, rather than taking time to spend time alone with God and pray. I was justifying my choice by thinking that I was working for God. But my work was not more important than spending time alone with Jesus. I foolishly ended up trying to do it all in my own strength when I already knew that I couldn't.

School and homework, although important, can also be distractions if they keep you from spending time in the Word. Sports and sports practice build character and discipline but can also take precedence over going to church. Thousands of families will invest almost every extra hour in getting their children to practice and spend every weekend at the motor cross track or at the baseball/softball field with a sincere desire to invest in their children, only to teach them that their distractions are more important than God.

I love fishing. It's probably good that I don't live near a body of water where I could spend every afternoon with a line in the water. Fishing is one of my favorite activities, but I must keep it in the right perspective. I am sure you have interests and hobbies that are important to you, too. If you're not careful, they can use up all the extra time you have after work and school.

This may sound funny coming from a pastor, but another thing that can distract us from God is serving in ministry. Everyone should be involved in the church but not at the expense of spending time with God. Last year I made the decision to be less involved in church and community activities because I was too busy. I needed to spend time with God, not just serve Him.

I have to remember that my work isn't so important that God needs me to do it. The truth is, God doesn't need me to do anything. He allows me to serve Him. Serving Him is a privilege. And so to think that I am too busy serving God to slow down to spend quite time with God is actually self-centered.

It is possible to let the "good" supersede the "best." Martha should have delayed the meal or made something simple and chosen to spend time with Jesus instead. If anyone had complained, Jesus would have defended her in the same way He defended her sister. Choose the best, good thing, or you may miss out on blessings or opportunities God has in store for you in the moment.

The time you spend with Jesus is not wasted time—it's vital time. It is vital to your spiritual maturity, it is vital to your understanding of Him, it is vital to the way you live your life and the fruit you produce. Choose to prioritize your activities so you can spend important time with God and not miss your connection with Him. Spending time and connecting with God is the best way to avoid walking in your own strength and wisdom away from Him and becoming vulnerable to the attacks of the enemy. Sit at the feet of Jesus, soaking in all that He has for you. In doing so, you will be equipped to face and overcome the fears and anxieties you may experience in life.

WORKBOOK

Chapter Two Questions

Question: What are some good things in your life that keep you from the best things? How can you find and maintain balance with how you choose to spend your time?

Question: Describe a time when you allowed serving God to replace a relationship with God. Why is this a particularly subtle temptation? How can you prioritize Jesus over ministry?

_____

_____

_____

_____

_____

_____

_____

_____

_____

_____

Question: Read in the gospels about Christ's devotional life. (See Matthew 4:1–11; Matthew 14:22–25; Matthew 26:36–44; Luke 6:12–13; Luke 9:28–36; Luke 11:1–4; John 17.) What do these passages teach about having intimate time with God each day? What other biblical and/or historical figures modeled this daily time with God?

_____

_____

_____

_____

_____

_____

_____

_____

_____

_____

Journal: As part of your daily time with God, find a quiet place and put away everything except your Bible and journal. Select a passage to read and use your journal to jot down a verse that stands out, a praise or prayer request on your heart, or other ways that God is speaking to you. Some people find it helpful to write out their prayers.

Action: Ask a mentor or leader in your church to meet with you and model/explain how they have a daily devotional time. Consider investing in a journal, prayer notebook, devotional, or study Bible.

Chapter Two Notes

CHAPTER THREE

Keep Your Eyes on Jesus

Immediately [Jesus] made the disciples get into the boat and go before him to the other side, while he dismissed the crowds. And after he had dismissed the crowds, he went up on the mountain by himself to pray. When evening came, he was there alone, but the boat by this time was a long way from the land, beaten by the waves, for the wind was against them. And in the fourth watch of the night he came to them, walking on the sea. But when the disciples saw him walking on the sea, they were terrified, and said, "It is a ghost!" and they cried out in fear. But immediately Jesus spoke to them, saying, "Take heart; it is I. Do not be afraid."
—Matthew 14:22–27

Jesus had just heard that John the Baptist had been beheaded, so He sailed to a desolate place where He could grieve and pray. But when He got there, a huge crowd was waiting for Him on the shore. When Jesus saw them, He had compassion on them. He healed many and taught them.

At the end of the day, five thousand people were stuck in the wasteland without anything to eat. Jesus fed them all with only five loaves of bread and two fish. Then He dismissed the crowd and sent the disciples to sail to the other side of the lake so He could finally be alone to pray. His disciples had just witnessed one of Jesus' greatest miracles, yet they still didn't fully understand who He was.

Sometime between three and six in the morning, after supernaturally seeing His disciples in the distance struggling in a life-threatening storm, Jesus went to His disciples.

When He arrived they had been struggling and rowing for over eight hours against hurricane force winds and huge waves a considerable distance from the shore. No problem. This was Jesus. The quickest way to reach the disciples was to walk to them on the water.

Picture it. It's dark and stormy outside, and the disciples are working hard. The weather is against them, and the boat is at risk of capsizing and sinking—a decidedly stressful moment. The disciples are soaked to the bone and exhausted from trying to stay alive. Then, out of nowhere, they see someone walking on the water.

Let that image sink in. They see someone in the middle of this storm calmly walking on the water! They think He's a ghost! Now, that may sound silly, but think about it. If you were alone late at night on a boat in the middle of a lake and saw someone walking on the water, you'd probably react the same way as the disciples.

Jesus tells them, "Take heart, it is I [literally I AM, see John 8:48–59; Exodus 3:13–14]. Do not be afraid." Their fears melt—it's the Master. The transition is immediate: one moment, these men are terrified because they think they see a ghost. When Jesus speaks they suddenly recognize that their Teacher, their Healer, their Leader is *God.* In fact, once Jesus climbs into the boat, the wind and waves immediately cease and Matthew tells us that they "worshiped him, saying, 'Truly you are the Son of God'" (Matthew 14:33).

The truth is that God's Word handles our fears. His Word had the power to calm the wind, the rain, and the raging sea, and it has the power to calm your fears. The Word of God can strengthen your heart. It can give you courage and hope. When Christ speaks, you can be confident in what He says to you. Here are some promises that can comfort your soul in times of trouble:

- "He will never leave you nor forsake you" (Deuteronomy 31:6 NIV).

- "Come to Me, all who are weary and heavy-laden, and I will give you rest" (Matthew 11:28–29 NASB).

- "Do not let your hearts be troubled. You believe in God; believe also in me. My Father's house has many rooms; if that were not so, would I have told you that I am going there to prepare a place for you? And if I go and prepare a place for you, I will come back and take you to be with me that you also may be where I am" (John 14:1–3 NIV).

- "My sheep hear my voice, and I know them, and they follow me. I give them eternal life, and they will never perish, and no one will snatch them out of my hand" (John 10:27–28).

The Distraction of Fear

The Words of Christ have the power to calm your fears and strengthen your heart. Peter even took it as step further, asking Jesus to let him walk on water, too.

> And Peter answered him, "Lord, if it is you, command me to come to you on the water." He said, "Come." So Peter got out of the boat and walked on the water and came to Jesus. But when he saw the wind, he was afraid, and beginning to sink he cried out, "Lord, save me." Jesus immediately reached out his hand and took hold of him, saying to him, "O you of little faith, why did you doubt?" And when they got into the boat, the wind ceased. And those in the boat worshiped him, saying, "Truly you are the Son of God."
> **—Matthew 14:28–33**

Peter trusted Jesus' word. When Jesus said, "Come," Peter didn't hesitate. He stepped right out of the boat, confident he could do what Jesus was doing. Peter believed he could walk on water because he trusted Christ's ability to help him.

Understand the powerful effect of Christ's words. Peter didn't just feel better about himself because of Jesus. He didn't just feel more hopeful, more satisfied, because Jesus was there. He stepped out of the boat and began to walk on water because of the words of Christ.

This must have been a thrilling experience for Peter. What a glorious moment! Everything is beautiful; life is good. It's perfect—as long as Peter has his attention fixed on Christ.

Have you ever experienced a time when you couldn't

do something, and then suddenly you could? It was a wonderful moment in my life when I could ride a bike! Do you remember struggling, falling, getting back on, wobbling, and falling again when you first attempted to ride a bike? And then one day, it just clicks, and you're riding your bike with ease. What an amazing moment. You may have had that experience with swimming or standing on your head or doing a cartwheel or hitting a baseball on the sweet spot of the bat! It must have been like that for Peter. He was walking on water!

But the thrill didn't last long because when Peter experienced the force of the waves around him, fear again caused him to lose sight of Christ. Immediately, he began to sink into the tumultuous waters. He had enough faith to walk on the water—something that nobody else has ever done—but his faith failed to keep him there when he became distracted by fear, so much so that Jesus said, "You of little faith."

It wasn't the last time this happened to Peter. In fact, the night before Jesus was crucified, Peter told Jesus boldly, "Lord, I am ready to go with you both to prison and to death" (Luke 22:33), and all the other disciples said the same (Matthew 26:33–35).

Peter believed with all his heart that he was going to follow Jesus wherever He went. But when Jesus got arrested and the disciples finally figured out that He was doomed, it all changed. Peter's fear began to well up in him and he realized he would be next! They were going to be looking for him. People connected to Jesus were in trouble and, once again, Peter let his fear distract him.

Peter lost sight of Christ and who He is. In Matthew

26:69–75, Peter denied three times that he even knew Jesus. He did not just say, "Hey, I don't know Him," but his denial was adamant. He cursed as he denied knowing Jesus, the Man with whom he'd spent three and a half years of his life, watching Him do what He did every day—perform miracles, walk on water, raise the dead. Peter denied the One to whom he had said: "You are the Christ, the Son of the living God" (Matthew 16:16).

Peter's fear caused him to lose sight of the strength and courage he had in Jesus. It railroaded his faith. And it can do the same to you.

Fear in Your Life

The circumstances of your life can begin to play on your fears and cause you to become anxious, worried, and lose sight of God and His power. Like Peter, you begin to sink and drown in your own emotions, replaying and questioning decisions you have made in faith. You fall prey to the negative consequences of fear. These consequences are very persistent.

You begin to worry, ruminate, and experience deep anxiety. You think about things over and over. You experience less joy and peace, and you find it hard to concentrate. Fear overwhelms your emotions.

Fear also affects your physical body. You lose sleep, don't eat, get fatigued, depressed, and anxious. Fear, anxiety, and worry are often linked to things like heart disease, strokes, migraines, gastrointestinal dysfunction, and many other health issues.[6] Many of these things need a doctor's care, and you should never ignore the symptoms.

Fear affects all your relationships. Many people find it hard to spend time with someone who's always worried, negative, fearful, and fatalistic. Fear and anxiety hamper your work relationships with your co-workers, your bosses, and your subordinates. People distracted by fear tend not to make solid decisions; they waffle and hesitate and get hung up in analysis paralysis. Fear can make it difficult to get anything done at work.

Anxiety impacts our relationships with our spouses and children. Parents who worry all the time tend to raise kids who worry all the time. Children whose parents struggle with fear tend to feel less secure and less loved.

Most importantly, your fears and worries divert attention away from Jesus to other things. They can distract you from the strength and the confidence you have in Christ. When you take your eyes off Jesus, you focus on the dilemma at hand. I think that's why the Bible tells us over and over and over again not to be afraid (Deuteronomy 1:29) or anxious (Philippians 4:6).

Fear may cause you to forget about God's faithfulness if you get cancer. You may lose sight of the fact that God is your Provider when the money runs low. Or you may forget that you're forgiven by the grace of God when you make a mistake or fall headlong into sin. Fear is a horrible distraction from your walk with God because it causes you to lose sight of the gospel. It causes you to try and walk in your own strength, and it makes you more susceptible to temptation, sin, and discouragement.

Categories of Fear

Fear is not always a bad thing. It can have a purpose when it is appropriate. For example, when you step off the curb onto the street and you hear a car horn, fear can motivate you to get back on the curb where you're safe. The right kind of fear can help you be prepared for emergencies or make you cautious when you're surrounded by people you don't know in an area you're not familiar. But there are other kinds of fears that are crippling and that overwhelm your life and distract you from all your relationships, especially your relationship with God.

Fears from the past. Maybe you did something wrong in the past—a crime, a betrayal, an act of unfaithfulness— and you're worried about getting caught. Maybe you did something you are ashamed of and you don't want anyone to find out. The fear of this becoming public is more than you can bear, so it eats away at you. Maybe someone who did you wrong in a relationship or in a business deal wants to talk about it in private.

Fear of current circumstances. Maybe you lost your dog or you're not sure if you'll get a good grade on an important test. Maybe you felt a lump where there wasn't supposed to be a lump. Maybe you have a child serving in the military in the Middle East from whom you haven't heard in a few days. Or you open the mail and find a bill you weren't expecting and realize there now isn't going to be enough money to buy groceries. Or you have a neighbor who has someone stopping by every fifteen minutes all night long, and you realize what's going on.

Our world is full of question marks, dangerous situations, and uncertainty, which can leave you so overwhelmed and fearful that you lose sight of your Savior and begin to drown in your anxiety.

Fear of the unknown. The future is full of unknowns, things you can't see, things that are beyond your ability to know and control. A quick way to identify this kind of fear is by asking, "What if?" You hear it all the time. What if the economy tanks? What if there's a government shutdown? What if you buy a new house but then lose your job? Or what if, heaven forbid, the Patriots win yet another Super Bowl?

Many people have debilitating fears of the unknown that can consume them and cause them incessant worry. Again, this kind of fear draws attention away from God and sidetracks you. Sometimes, it's pervasive enough to require medical attention.

Fear of the unknown causes you to lose sight of His ability to take care of you and the promises He has made, like the promise that He works all things for the good of those who love Him and are called according to His purpose (Romans 8:28). Another promise states that "he who began a good work in you will bring it to completion at the day of Jesus Christ" (Philippians 1:6). It is also encouraging and empowering to remember that "if God is for us, who can be against us?" (Romans 8:31).

The modern world seems to be steadily growing darker, at least in the Western world. Fear of the unknown and the other destructive categories of fear can cause you to lose sight of the sovereignty and the power of God, which is really the issue.

A Need for Control

Your fears are rooted in trying to control what you cannot control. That's really the heart of fear. You want to control the past, your current circumstances, and the unknown, but you are not in control.

Stop right where you are and acknowledge this truth: *you are not in control.*

You're not in control of the weather, the economy, or even your own kids. You're not in control of elections, or Syria, or what Russia does in response. You're not in control of the traffic on the freeway. You can't control cancer, the planetary alignments, gravity, the wind, or the pace of technology. If you're honest, you'll admit that at times, you can't even control yourself!

Your fears also stem from a misplaced trust. This probably smarts a little bit, but fear tends to be a sign that you're trusting in something other than God. There's a reason why the Bible says, "Trust in the LORD with *all* your heart, and do not lean on your own understanding" (Proverbs 3:5, emphasis added). You may find yourself trusting your intuition, your ability to figure things out on your own, other people, or the government. But God alone, the Creator of the entire universe, is in control. He is sovereign. All things are within His power and will. Stop trusting in other things more than you trust in God.

Fear is debilitating. It distracts you from God and is rooted in your desire to control what you can't.

So how do you overcome fear and keep it at bay?

Spend time in prayer and apply yourself to seeking the truth in the Word of God. It's about time with Him.

Remember that God's sanctifying work is not done yet. You are broken and live in a broken world full of broken sinners, so you will probably at times fall into fear and worry; you will lose sight of Christ at moments when the troubles around you begin to overwhelm you.

When that happens cry out, "Lord save me from my fear! Save me from my doubts! Strengthen my heart, turn my eyes back to you." Cry out to Jesus. He will reach out His hand and take hold of you. He will steady you and strengthen you and set your feet back firmly on the rock (Psalm 40:2).

Keep your eyes fixed on Jesus, and your fears, doubts, and worries will begin to fade into the background of the glorious grace that He has for you. Your fear should instantly remind you to immediately turn to Christ, because that is where your hope is. No matter if you are facing the unknown of the economy, the results of an MRI, or the loss of someone you love. Jesus is your anchor in the storms of life and He will not fail you. Turn to Him.

Sometimes your distractions go beyond fears and anxieties or even the everyday disruptions of modern living. In the next chapter, we'll change gears a little bit and talk about distractions that you may not even realize exist— your personal assumptions about life.

WORKBOOK

Chapter Three Questions

Question: Describe a time when your fears were relieved by the presence of the Lord. How did you recognize His presence in the situation and how did your awareness of His presence change your perspective?

Question: What are some of the external circumstances (wind and waves) that are causing fear in your life right now? What are the consequences of that fear in your emotional and physical health, as well as in your relationships with God and others?

_____

_____

_____

_____

_____

_____

_____

_____

_____

_____

Question: Look at the fears you listed above. What are you trying to control? Where have you misplaced your trust?

_____

_____

Journal: How are you doing with your daily appointment with God? It is impossible to overemphasize how important this is in your life. Only time in prayer, reading and meditating on the Word, and spending time in worship will help you grow in your relationship with God and overcome your fears. As you have your time with God, journal about your fears and ask Him for His peace.

Like Peter, cry out to Jesus when you are sinking. Ask Him to save you from your fear and doubts and turn your eyes back to Him. He will reach out His hand and take hold of you. He will steady and strengthen you and set your feet back firmly on the rock.

Action: For each of the fears you listed, find an appropriate Bible verse that combats your fear. Write, memorize, and meditate on them. Start with Matthew 6:25–33 for a passage about fear and worry in general.

Chapter Three Notes

CHAPTER FOUR

The Truth and Your Assumptions

The most unrecognized and subtle distractions in your life are not technology, work, hobbies, or obsessing about your 401k. The most subtle and unseen distractions in your life are your faulty assumptions.

We all have assumptions, which are preconceived ideas that color our perceptions of the world around us. You make assumptions about people, about how the world works, about simple things like light switches (e.g., up is on, down is off). When you go to the gas station and put your credit card in, you assume your bank is still in business and your money is still there. When you put the gas nozzle in your car, you assume you're going to get gas in your tank and not root beer. Simple. You don't even think about it.

You also make assumptions about very complex things that you don't truly understand, like gravity. Every time you take a step, you assume that the force of gravity is going to work exactly as it has before. You also assume that when you sit down in a chair it will hold you up.

Some of our assumptions may be fairly certain, like the assumption about gravity, but others may not be so certain, like your bank account—especially if you're not balancing your checkbook every day.

Assumptions can profoundly influence your life and family. For example, what you assume about your children and how they think will influence how you treat them. If you assume your kids are always up to no good, you will probably watch them like a hawk. If you assume that your kids never do anything wrong, you will be inclined to give them too much latitude.

What you assume about how your spouse thinks and acts will influence how you behave with them. If you assume your husband to be a self-centered, inconsiderate jerk, you just may be prone to nag. If you assume your wife doesn't do anything all day while you are at work, you will be prone to ignore the evidence that taking care of you and the kids is the biggest job.

Your assumptions influence your view of politics. You can assume the best about people or the worst about people. Some individuals assume everyone is a racist or that everyone else is stupid. At that point, discussion stops. Everyone just lives out their assumptions.

Your assumptions affect how you relate to others—for good and for bad. They affect what you believe about your work and how you approach it. If your assumption is that the company doesn't like you or care about you, your work ethic is probably going to be a little weak, but if you believe you're valued and taken care of, you work harder.

Some assumptions are well founded based on good

information or solid experience, like the law of gravity or a well-managed checkbook. Some are based on misinformation or incomplete information, such as moral relativism that is founded on the idea that there is no absolute standard of truth. Some are based on mixed signals from others, and some are based on plain old ignorance or false teaching.

Flawed Assumptions About God

When it comes to how you think about God, it is possible to have deeply flawed assumptions about who He is and what He is doing in your life. This is certainly the case with people who don't know God—atheists, agnostics, and individuals pursuing false religions. It can also be true for believers—people who have a saving relationship with Christ or have at least made a profession of faith in Jesus. That's what this chapter is about: faulty assumptions. It is a fact that faulty assumptions displace the truth, thereby damaging your relationship with God and His people. Let's look at the book of Matthew, using Peter again as our example.

> From that time Jesus began to show his disciples that he must go to Jerusalem and suffer many things from the elders and chief priests and scribes, and be killed, and on the third day be raised. And Peter took him aside and began to rebuke him, saying, "Far be it from you, Lord! This shall never happen to you." But he turned and said to Peter, "Get behind me, Satan! You are a hindrance to me. For you are not setting your mind on the things of God, but on the things of man."
>
> **—Matthew 16:21–23**

This interchange with Jesus reveals that Peter's problem was that Peter assumed his vision of the future was the same as God's. He assumed that his program was God's program and that his plans were God's plans. Now Peter had some things right: he believed Jesus was the Messiah, the Son of God, and he believed Jesus was the one everyone had been waiting for to come and make things right. However, he had a lot of wrong assumptions about how Jesus would do that.

Like virtually all observant Jews of his time, Peter assumed that the Messiah would deliver Israel from her oppressors. Remember, the Jews had been subjugated by the Assyrians, the Babylonians, the Persians, the Greeks, and now the Romans, as well as many Canaanite tribes throughout their history. They thought their Messiah would end this oppression, expel the Roman government and all its troops by force, and establish Israel as a dominant power once again. Peter believed that Jesus would lead that revolt personally and literally ascend to King David's throne and reign over Israel forever and ever.

Peter may have even believed that since he was close to Jesus, he would be second in command. He assumed Jesus would be a conquering king, not a suffering servant. Peter was so wrong.

When Jesus said He would be tortured and killed and raised to new life, Peter rebuked Him because that picture didn't fit with his assumptions. Jesus was trying to prepare His disciples for what was about to happen, but Peter wasn't even listening to Him anymore. In his own mind, Peter had it all figured out and he merely rejected the truth. Peter was shaping his view of Christ by his own assumptions and his preconceived ideas instead of drawing his conclusions from the Word of God that Jesus spoke.

Before you say, "Well that's really dumb," understand that many people assume that their plans are God's plans. In fact, making flawed assumptions is a major distraction for Christians. It may be that your view of God is shaped by your assumptions, rather than your assumptions—your thinking—being shaped by the Word of God.

Assumptions are often formed by your culture, upbringing, church traditions, emotions, and experiences . Your view of God can become man-centered instead of God-centered. That's what Jesus said to Peter: "You are not setting your mind on the things of God, but on the things of man" (Matthew 16:23). You're not looking at things from God's perspective; you're looking at them from man's perspective. Your mind and heart are not set on things of God, but on the things that you want and the way you want things to go.

Jesus even named what was behind Peter's wrong thinking: Satan. The enemy stokes your fears, worries, anxieties, and faulty assumptions. Behind them all, you find your enemy and God's enemy. Satan constantly works to harm your relationship with God and dim God's glory.

The enemy does his part—with his whispers, half-truths, and accusations—and all too often, you do your part by listening and believing. It doesn't matter how long you've been walking with Jesus or how spiritually mature you think you are—you're susceptible. Satan is extremely crafty and doesn't play by the rules.

Think about it: Peter spent three years walking along-side Jesus *in person*. Peter was the first to clearly acknowledge and recognize that Jesus was the long-awaited promised Messiah. Yet Peter was rebuked by that very same Messiah when his assumptions hindered Jesus' ministry.

Your assumptions are significant. When your faulty assumptions manifest in your thoughts, words, and behavior, you become an actual hindrance to the ministry of Jesus on earth. You can see this throughout American Christianity. Many people who claim to follow Christ tend to have their hearts and minds set on man-centered ideas. Those people may not even recognize that those ideas are false assumptions, but those lies have permeated every area of their lives.

However, these false assumptions can be shattered when your mind is rooted in the Word of God. Only the truth from the Bible can keep you from being led into false assumptions about who God is. Paul wrote that "all Scripture is breathed out by God and profitable for teaching, for reproof, for correction, and for training in righteousness, that the man of God may be complete, equipped for every good work" (2 Timothy 3:16–17).

As you grow in your maturity in Christ, the Bible says you will not be "tossed to and fro by the waves and carried about by every wind of doctrine, by human cunning, by craftiness in deceitful schemes" (Ephesians 4:14). When you root out the false assumptions in your own mind and heart, you will be better equipped to discern the false teachings distracting many churches today. We will tackle this subject in the next chapter.

WORKBOOK

Chapter Four Questions

Question: Have you ever had a moment like Peter where you felt God was not doing things the right way? What faulty assumptions had you made? How did God set you straight?

Question: Look at these three main sources of assumptions: culture, upbringing, and experiences. How has each influenced you and the people around you? Have you adopted the assumptions of close friends or family without really thinking them through to determine if they are biblically accurate?

_____

_____

_____

_____

_____

_____

_____

_____

_____

_____

Question: What is the best way to reveal your assumptions about life and about God and to correct them so that they line up with truth?

_____

_____

_____

_____

_____

_____

_____

_____

_____

_____

_____

_____

Journal: During your daily time with God, write down false assumptions you have made about God and how they have affected your relationship with Him. Repent and ask for God's forgiveness and ask Him to help you overcome this wrong thinking. For each assumption, provide Scripture that dispels the false idea. Remember that assumptions may have taken a lifetime to form and will not usually disappear overnight.

Action: How can you broaden your perspective as a Christian? How can you learn from believers in other cultures, from different backgrounds, or in different life callings? Make a conscious decision to read, listen to, or get to know believers outside your normal circles who also hold up God's Word as the standard for absolute truth and who avoid the distractions talked about in the next chapter. Ask God to help break down your unbiblical or untrue assumptions and to give you a heart set on Him.

Chapter Four Notes

_____

_____

_____

_____

_____

_____

_____

_____

_____

_____

_____

_____

_____

_____

_____

_____

_____

_____

_____

_____

_____

_____

CHAPTER FIVE

The Distracted Church

The enemy is determined to wipe out the truth of the gospel and the salvation of mankind. He hates us. In the very beginning of the book of Genesis, we find his cunning at work. He said to the woman, "Did God actually say, 'You shall not eat of any tree in the garden'?" (Genesis 3:1). The doubt Satan cast in the mind of Eve brought the curse of sin on all of us.

Satan floods the church with his lies and distortions, hoping to drown us all with his deception. And, unfortunately, sometimes it works. It is difficult for the body of Christ to navigate all the pitfalls and faulty assumptions that the world has embraced. We want to be liked and accepted by the world, but we forget that Jesus told us that for His sake we would be hated. The following examples discuss some ways the modern church and many believers have been distracted from the truth of God's Word and bought into the plan of evil.

The Prosperity Gospel

The prosperity gospel assumes that God's purpose for creating you was to make you healthy, wealthy, and prosperous. It suggests that God brought you into a relationship with Him to prosper you on the earth beyond your imagination, so you can have all your material desires fulfilled—if you just have enough faith.

These claims are not in line with the truth of the Bible. The Bible teaches that you were created and saved for the glory of God. He saved you because He loves you and sacrificed Himself for you, but, ultimately, this life is about His glory, not your material prosperity in this life. The purpose of your life is the same purpose He has for everything else—to bring Him glory. God says in the book of Isaiah, "Bring my sons from afar and my daughters from the end of the earth, everyone who is called by my name, whom I created for my glory, whom I formed and made" (Isaiah 43:6–7).

Moreover, God does not promise to give you a lot of wealth or an easy life just because you have faith in Him. He promises other, more important things: salvation from your sins (1 John 1:7), a future hope and eternity with Him (John 3:16), to strengthen you when this life gets hard (2 Corinthians 12:9), and to never leave you or forsake you (Hebrews 13:5). He never promised a pain-free, problem-free life.

In fact, Jesus actually assured us of something entirely different: He promised that life is going to be hard. He said, "I have said these things to you, that in me you may have peace. In the world you will have tribulation. But take heart; I have overcome the world" (John 16:33). Notice He didn't say you may have tribulation, but rather, He said you *will* have tribulation.

Paul tells us: "Indeed, all who desire to live a godly life in Christ Jesus will be persecuted" (2 Timothy 3:12).

Everyone who wants to follow God will experience difficulty. Jesus said in the Sermon on the Mount, "Blessed are the poor in spirit … blessed are those who mourn … blessed are those who are persecuted" (Matthew 5:3–4, 10). The Bible does not promise that if you believe in Jesus, all your problems will magically go away and everything will be perfect. He only promises that He has satisfied the wrath of God for you, will be with you through it all, and will then bring you safely home to be with Him if you trust in Him.

The prosperity gospel is based on a man-centered assumption—a desire to be rich—and not on the Word of God. It's a belief system that is flawed and leaves you empty because it's based on a false assumption that the gift is greater than the Giver of the gift. People come to the prosperity gospel because they want the gifts, but they don't want the Giver. When you finally realize that the greatest gift you can receive is the Giver Himself, then everything else fades in comparison.

Legalism

Legalism is a man-centered view that assumes, maybe subconsciously, that God's approval is ultimately about your behavior—what you do or do not do for Him. This can be a little harder to detect because it's possible to fall into legalism with good intentions and without even recognizing it yourself. In fact, you affirm that you are saved by grace through faith in Christ alone. You assert that salvation isn't by works but by faith in Christ's atoning work on the cross. However, slowly, as legalism creeps into your life, you begin to change.

Legalism is an assumption that subtly attaches itself to the gospel. Legalism whispers, *"Yes, you're saved by grace, but you also need to stop doing this and start doing that."* Say you were someone who used to struggle with alcohol, but you stopped drinking and found victory. Praise the Lord! But you may then begin to think, *"All true Christians never drink."*

Or perhaps you've overcome lust in your heart by cutting out things like R-rated movies and secular music, so you think that means all Christians must forsake these things as well. Maybe you got saved in a church where everybody gets dressed up for service. Pretty soon you start believing all churches need to look that way. It's not always a conscious development, but in your mind the list grows until you're judging yourself and everyone else based upon a manmade checklist or set of traditions.

Don't misunderstand me: I firmly believe that when you're saved, your life is going to change. You cannot encounter the Creator of the universe without changing. You'll begin to bear fruit of that salvation. You'll begin to love God and love what He loves and hate the things He hates—sin in all its forms.

However, your ability to stop sinning is not the prerequisite for your salvation. Praise the Lord for that! Faith in Christ is the prerequisite. The grace of God is what saves us. Your ability to keep yourself from sin is not the prerequisite for staying saved either. That's due to the faithfulness of God.

Legalism assumes that there's something you need to do to make God love you and approve of you. It says you need to do something to prove you're saved. The Bible teaches that there's nothing—*nothing*—you can do to save yourself. The proof of your salvation ultimately is the grace-driven change in your life brought about by God. It is turning to Him and trusting Him more and more to mold you into His image.

Sentimentality

Sentimentality is the other end of the spectrum. It assumes that because God is love, no one is in trouble. God is not really just. No matter what you do or what your view of sin is, it doesn't matter because God is a loving God. He's not going to commit anybody to hell, regardless of what the Bible says about sin and depravity.

A sentimentality viewpoint of the gospel is built on faulty assumptions, driven by emotion. I understand the prospect of hell is horrid. The thought of anyone spending eternity in torment should cause you to shudder and grieve. Knowing that there are people who every day step off into eternity without knowing Christ should be something that stirs you to tears and prompts you to share the gospel.

As horrible as this reality is, it is still the truth, though many people simply don't want to believe it. At the root of their false assumption is the belief that God's attribute of love is the only one that counts. If that is what you believe, your concept of love is flawed and not in line with what the Bible teaches. God's ways are higher than your ways. God is not only love, but also utterly holy, righteous, and just. Therefore, unredeemed man will be punished for his sin. Justice demands as much. God is a God of amazing mercy and grace, but also of overwhelming wrath and true justice.

The New Testament mentions hell twenty-three times, and seventeen of those are quotes from Jesus. He talked about hell more than heaven. Why? Because hell is the tougher one to hear about, but it's equally important.

The Bible teaches that for God to be love, He must also be just—otherwise, His love is just sentimentality.[7] By the same token, if God's going to be just, He must also be love—otherwise, His justice is brutality.[8] God has to be both. It is who He is, so the sentimental view of Him is faulty, based on false assumptions.

If there's something in our culture that's sending people to hell, it is this view right here: that there is no hell. It tells people, "You're going to be fine." More and more Christians have bought into this idea to their doom.

Unhealthy Mysticism

Let's face it, God the Holy Spirit coming to live inside of you, lead you, guide you, convict you of your sin, reveal the truth found in the Word of God, and illuminate your mind, is a mystical experience. This is something that goes beyond head knowledge and intellectual assent. John Piper calls this kind of relationship with God "rational and supra-rational."[9] In short, we as Christians can experience in this life the presence and power of the living One true God. Through prayer and biblical meditation on the Word, God opens our spiritual eyes to be able to behold and understand the truth and the glory of God. This concept is also known as Christian mysticism.

Mysticism might sound foreign, mysterious, or even cultic, but that is because we tend to, by assumption, equate the term with Eastern mysticism. Christian mysticism is something altogether different. For the sake of this book, let me define Christian mysticism as an internal, often emotional, experience with God.

D. D. Martin is a bit more technical in his article in the *Evangelical Dictionary of Theology*. He writes, "Christian mysticism seeks to describe an experienced, direct, non-abstract, unmediated, loving knowledge of God, a knowing or seeing so direct as to be called union with God."[10] This information is heavy, I know, and there is a lot more to this that can be covered here. Suffice it is to say, it is a personal experience with God that can be hope-inspiring, joy-giving, and faith-strengthening. However, it is ultimately subjective. This is where many Christians and churches fall off the rails.

For many, mysticism is the assumption that feelings, intuition, and religious experiences are definitively God's voice. Unhealthy mysticism is when your thoughts and feelings become the authority in your life, equal to or greater than the Word of God—when you focus on what you sense internally rather than on what God says objectively. People who have never read the Bible may say, "God spoke to me."

Nowhere in the Bible does it suggest that you should do or believe anything from inside you based simply on your feelings and emotions. Nowhere. In fact, we are sternly warned about the deceitfulness of our own hearts (Jeremiah 17:9).

Over and over the Bible exhorts you to believe what God says. Any intuition or feeling that does not line up with the inerrant Word of God is not to be trusted, whether it's a burning feeling in your chest or a dream or a sense of peace, an audible voice from heaven, or even an angel standing next to your bed. If what you heard does not line up with Scripture, it's a false assumption.

I know a couple of different men who in the last year have told me, "I believe it's God's will that I leave my wife and move on. I've found a peace about that." Seriously!

I tried to explain to them that it's not His voice that they are hearing! It is their own emotions justifying something they want to do, rather than working through any problems in their marriage. The Word of God is clear about this issue. It is not God's will for man to leave his wife. Jesus made an exception when it comes to sexual infidelity, but even then He never said you must leave in such cases, or even that you should—only that you could.

I'm not saying God never speaks to His people or intervenes in your life. In fact, my own testimony is that God intervened in my life in a way that I couldn't deny His existence. I had a very real experience with God. In the beginning, He spoke to my heart about a horrific sin I was about to commit. Soon after, I went to a Bible study and heard the gospel and I believed.

Since then, my whole life has been about learning, understanding, and believing the Word, not just about my feelings. At times I've believed God has led me somewhere or to do something, but I always confirm it with the Word of God. He does prompt, nudge and push, but the primary way He speaks is in the Scriptures, and if what you feel doesn't line up with that, then it's wrong.

Let me give you a litmus tests regarding God's leading: if your feelings contradict Scripture, your feelings are not of God. It's that simple. Always check your feelings, intuitions, and religious experiences by the Word of God. If you believe God is speaking to you but you have never read the Bible, the chances are very good that you might be wrong.

You must get in the Word and check your inclination against God's Word. Unhealthy mysticism can be a very big distraction and lead you down the wrong path if you are not vigilant to study and learn God's Word and confirm your intuition with it.

Consumerism

Consumerism is probably the most subtle assumption of all, because it's the American way. You live in a country with a free-market economy driven by customer satisfaction. I'm not saying this is bad, especially when it comes to buying goods and services. If you buy something that doesn't work, you go back to the company you bought it from. If they treat you badly you just go somewhere else. This attitude applies to TV shows, restaurants, cars, clothes, homes, etc. Everything must conform to your need, your budget, and your taste. Consumerism creates a certain satisfaction, but it has infiltrated theology, especially regarding the church.

For many Americans, individualism is considered a virtue. Consumerism says that your church experience is about coming to a place where you consume a worship experience, therefore you have the right to decide whether you like it or not. You may think church is about you, your likes, preferences, and feelings.

Your church should fit the image that you want to project to others. So you shop around for a church like you do for a new shirt or restaurant. You evaluate the music, the people, the style, the length of service, the Bible translation used, the seating—all according to your preferences. There are even sermon reviews on Twitter to help you assess a pastor's teaching in advance.

Now, instead of focusing on leading their congregation to truth, pastors are worried about reviews. I know this from personal experience. Somebody recently gave our church a two-star review on Google because he thought I was judgmental for telling the truth.

However, in reality, none of this packaging matters. Does a church focus on preaching the Word of God? Is the gospel being proclaimed? Are people growing in their individual walks with Christ? True worship is more important than the music style. The Word of God says church is about getting plugged into a body of believers that have been built up and are becoming more like Christ (1 Corinthians 14:12). That's what changes lives. That's what church is for, but so many people choose and leave churches based on consumerist ideals.

Church isn't about getting something you like, but rather about receiving something you need. It is not an experience that tickles your fancy, but one that feeds the Word of God to your soul.

You need to lift up your voice and passionately proclaim your love for Christ. You need to connect with your brothers and sisters and encourage each other to be built up and strengthened so you can go into the world and do what God is calling you to do. You need to get your marching orders and take the fight to the enemy, because the gates of hell are not supposed to stand against us (Matthew 16:18).

How do you do that? The answer is to keep your minds set on Christ. You need to saturate your mind with Jesus. Or as Colossians 3:1–2 says, "If then you have been raised with Christ, seek the things that are above, where Christ is, seated at the right hand of God. Set your minds on things that are above, not on things that are on earth."

The Apostle Paul said:

> *And he gave the apostles, the prophets, the evangelists, the shepherds and teachers, to equip the saints for the work of ministry, for building up the body of Christ, until we all attain to the unity of the faith and of the knowledge of the Son of God.*
>
> *—Ephesians 4:11–13*

If you fall prey to the false teachings prevalent in many churches, you will find yourself distracted from your walk with God. You must repent and reject false teachings and find a church that teaches the unadulterated truth of the gospel (2 Corinthians 11:3–4, 12–15). When you remove false assumptions from your own life and are a part of an edifying body of Christ, you will be encouraged to pursue God wholly and to keep Him as your first love above all else.

WORKBOOK

Chapter Five Questions

Question: In what ways have you been distracted by the prosperity gospel teaching that God wants you to have health, wealth, and unlimited temporal blessings? What is your response to disappointment and suffering? Which is greater—your concern for God's glory or for your comfort?

_____

_____

Question: Do you tend more toward legalism or sentimentality? How can a reaction to one cause a swing to the
other? How can a Christian find and maintain a biblical
balance?

_____

_____

_____

_____

_____

_____

_____

_____

_____

_____

Question: How have you seen mysticism displayed in
popular Christian books or by well-known Christian
speakers? Describe a time when you or someone you
know tried to "Christianize" your feelings to justify that
they were God's will. What did you learn from that experience? How can you avoid mistaking your feelings for

God's leading as you move forward?

_____

_____

_____

_____

_____

_____

_____

_____

_____

_____

_____

_____

Journal: During your time with God, seriously and carefully consider the false assumptions being taught in the modern church. Purpose to study what the Bible says about prosperity, legalism, sentimentalism, mysticism, etc., either in your devotional time or through an in-depth Bible study. As you read God's Word daily, meditate on it and become a doer of the Word (James 1:22). You will grow alert to untruths being taught even by well-known Christian leaders or ministries.

Action: How do many churches fuel consumerism by their marketing strategies? Talk with a mentor or trusted Christian leader about what to look for in a church. What are some biblical criteria for when a person should join or leave a church?

Chapter Five Notes

_____

_____

_____

_____

_____

_____

_____

_____

_____

_____

_____

_____

_____

_____

_____

_____

_____

_____

_____

_____

_____

_____

CHAPTER SIX

Idols of the Heart

Martin Luther, regarded by many as the father of the Protestant Reformation, was a Roman Catholic monk for many years.[11] He was a brilliant student. As a monk in the sixteenth century, he had memorized the entire book of Psalms (in Latin), many other chunks of Scripture, and all of the church's teachings on sin and obedience.

Luther was devoted to following the Bible and the church's instructions scrupulously. He served obediently. He studied with zeal. He said the right prayers at the right time. He confessed every conceivable sin and asked forgiveness for not confessing the ones hidden even to himself. In short, he did everything he was supposed to do in order to remain in the good graces of both his superiors and God Almighty. He yearned for God to love him, to forgive him, and to accept him as His own.

However, he felt that what he was doing wasn't working. The more religious he became—the more he tried to make himself right with God by his own efforts—the more he realized he was lost and confused.

In his despair, Luther searched the Scriptures until he found the answer to his prayers for understanding:

> *For I am not ashamed of the gospel, for it is the power of God for salvation to everyone who believes, to the Jew first and also to the Greek. For in it the righteousness of God is revealed from faith for faith, as it is written, "The righteous shall live by faith."*
>
> **—Romans 1:16–17**

All those years of striving, self-denial, and mental anguish crystalized into the solution that had been before Luther all along: salvation is by faith alone! It is the gift of God. Luther only had to see it.

The Wrong Priority

More than a millennium earlier, a certain rich, young man was trying hard too. He took his case to Jesus, asking, "Teacher what good deed must I do to have eternal life?" (Matthew 19:16). When Jesus told the young man he needed to keep the commandments, the young man responded, "All these I have kept" (Matthew 19:20). In the account of this story in Luke 18, the passage includes that he said, "All these I have kept *from my youth*" (Luke 18:21, emphasis added).

But, like Luther, the man knew he was still missing something. He truly longed to know what that was. "What do I still lack?" (Matthew 19:20). Becoming a better rule follower was not the way for him to gain eternal life. The answer to his problem continued to elude him.

The young man thought he was following God, that by keeping the rules he could be right with Him. Jesus didn't want to give him false hope, so He answered in a way that got to the heart of the issue: "If you would be perfect..." (Matthew 19:21). Jesus wasn't talking about perfect behavior but about being *complete* and attaining the goal of eternal life.

Now it may surprise you, but Jesus didn't simply tell him, "Put your faith in Me. Repent of your sins and trust in Me for salvation." That is what you might expect as a good evangelical—because that's the gospel. Instead Jesus addressed the core issue. Jesus said to him, "If you would be perfect, go, sell what you possess and give to the poor, and you will have treasure in heaven; and come, follow me" (Matthew 19:21).

Why did Jesus tell him to do that? Selling all your possessions is not what gets you into heaven. Giving money to the poor isn't the way to get into heaven. You should absolutely be generous, but that doesn't win you eternal life. So what was His point? Jesus had talked about this issue before. He said:

Do not lay up for yourselves treasures on earth, where moth and rust destroy and where thieves break in and steal, but lay up for yourselves treasures in heaven, where neither moth nor rust destroys and where thieves do not break in and steal. For where your treasure is, there your heart will be also.

—Matthew 6:19–21

While the man standing before Jesus might have kept the rules, the problem was that his heart resided someplace else. It was not set on heaven; it was set on earthly things. He may have thought that heaven was what he wanted, but that wasn't where his real treasure was.

He had the wrong motives, the wrong ideas about his life with God. There was something in him that prevented him from surrendering himself to God and His purposes. Jesus was calling him to unburden himself of earthly riches so he could be free to devote himself to heavenly reward.

The young man finally understood what Jesus meant, but he turned and sadly walked away. He was sorrowful, almost weeping, for he must have recognized that he loved his earthly treasures more than he loved God (Matthew 19:22). He couldn't follow Jesus. Following Jesus would cost him more than he was willing to pay. He just couldn't do it. He had a heart problem.

A Heart Problem

He wasn't the only one. Jesus already had people close to Him who weren't saved. Think about Judas. Judas was with Jesus throughout His earthly ministry. He ate with Jesus. He traveled with Jesus. He watched Jesus perform miracles—heal the sick, walk on water, cast out demons, raise the dead. At some point Judas probably said, "I believe in Jesus. I believe He is the Messiah, the Son of God." But make no mistake, Judas was not saved. Something was seriously wrong with his heart.

There were others as well. When Jesus taught that He

was the Bread of Life, it offended a lot of people. By this He was announcing that He was the Messiah, the promised manna from heaven, and many of His followers stopped following Him (John 6:32–66). These were so called disciples, people who said they believed His teaching and witnessed His miracles. They thought they were saved, but they weren't.

What they really wanted was Jesus' miracles—His healing, His personal attention. They deserted Jesus because their hearts weren't changed, and because of that they couldn't go where Jesus was leading.

A Heart Change

Jesus didn't come to change your behavior but to change your heart. Your broken relationship with God isn't about your faulty behavior; it's about your sinful heart. You can modify your behavior, follow all the rules and regulations, but still your heart can be full of pride, envy, bitterness, greed, lust, hatred, and selfishness (Mark 7:21–23). Inwardly, you may be drawn to sin and rebellion.

You become distracted from God if you value or love anything above Him. When you want material objects more than you want Him, His presence in your life grows dim. You lose connection to Him and revert to living life in your own strength and your own ways.

There's another consequence to consider—idolatry. Idolatry is defined as the worship of physical objects or images as gods.[12] The early church father Origen wrote: "What each one honors before all else, what before all things he admires and loves, this for him is God."[13]

Distractions can lead to a disconnection from God. They lead you to put your hope in things other than God and can be become idols when they hinder your walk with Him.

Material Idols

In the Scripture story above, the young man's wealth had become an idol to him. He valued it so much he was willing to walk away from eternal life. This idolatry led him to reject Christ and the offer of eternity. What a devastating consequence!

I've talked about Christ to friends whose response to me was that they weren't interested because they didn't want to give up certain things in their life. Their idolatry kept them from a saving relationship with Christ.

However, idolatry doesn't always involve rejection of the gospel. It's not a sin reserved only for those who decide to worship false gods, individuals who feel that Christianity is stupid, or heretics. Even believers who have a deep faith in Christ can temporarily fall into idolatry.

Our hearts are fickle. You're saved by grace—without question—but still fallen and broken. You're capable of some pretty bad things, since you are still a sinner in the process of sanctification. God's not done with you yet.

More than that, you live in a world that's also broken and around people who are very broken. Thousands of things and people are competing for your time, attention, and affection, screaming, "Pay attention to me! Love me!

Care for me!"

Many things, such as money and material possessions, can draw your heart away from God. It can happen quickly. It's very easy to fall in love with money and possessions. They are always screaming for attention. Can you imagine saying no to a raise you have been offered?

The same thing that happened to the rich young man in Scripture can happen to you. Before you say that it's never going to happen to you, consider this: how much of your stuff, your money, or your possessions do you give away?

I'm not talking about the stuff you don't use any more, like that busted lawnmower or that closet full of clothes you can't even wear. I don't mean the junk you feel guilty about throwing away, so you have to find someone to give it to. I'm talking about regular, sacrificial giving, intentional generosity—the kind of giving that demonstrates that God is more important to you than your money.

What percentage of your resources do you give away? Ten percent? Five? Half a percent, maybe less? Don't get me wrong, I'm not beating you up here. This is a question for you to examine your own heart.

I'm just trying to help you see how quickly money and material possessions can become idols. They can draw you more and more away from God. We're all susceptible to it, including me. That's why regular percentage giving is important in the life of a Christian.

My wife and I have devoted a specific percentage amount of my paycheck to give away the moment it hits the bank, because I do not want money to be something that pulls at my heart. Give it away without hesitation, without even thinking about it. It demonstrates to the Lord that He is first in your heart, not your money. He gets the first portion of what you earn, because He is more important than the stuff that money can buy.

If you give grudgingly then you know where your heart is. The truth is, if you are not giving regularly somewhere and you use most of your resources on yourself, then your greatest love may not be God. It might be your stuff.

Relational Idols

Relationships can also become idols. If anything can compete with your affection for God, it's your affection for other people—spouses, children, parents, grandchildren, friends, heroes. Your heart can gravitate toward them and away from God.

If you set your priorities right, there's plenty of love to go around. You can love God and all the people in your life with deep affection. Take care to maintain a proper balance though, and protect your relationship to the Lord as well as important individuals.

You might think that sounds kind of weird. But consider this. Have you known people who claimed to be Christians, who seemed to be walking with God sincerely, but then began to hang out with a new crowd of people with a different set of values?

Then slowly, over time, they began to change. They became more like their new friends, and eventually, God was not in the picture anymore. They might have said they were still Christian, but they were no longer plugged in to a church, nor did they spend time with God. They allowed their relationship with other people to become primary over their relationship with God, which is the very definition of idolatry.

This outcome is unfortunate because it is certainly not wrong for Christians to love and spend time with people who have different values, as long as the Christians keep their relationship with God at the center of their life and heart. When Christ is their priority, Christians have the ability to really love others, and they can become a light of the gospel in the lives of their new friends.

However, sometimes our relationships with other people are so important to us that we don't want to risk those relationships by sharing the gospel. Perhaps you love God deeply but refrain from telling your loved ones the truth about sin and the salvation Christ offers. You may neglect to share the hope of the gospel with the people you love because you don't want to be rejected.

Never compromise the truth and power of the gospel just because you don't want to be at odds with someone you love. True love begins with God. If you truly love God and truly love others, you will keep Him first in your heart and you will share His truth with others.

A very good friend told me about an experience he had witnessing to someone who was a faithful member of a religious movement that identifies as Christian but denies the historical doctrines of the Christian faith. My friend was on fire for the Lord and ready to share Christ with this man. He came prepared every day by reading and studying the Word so he could answer this man's questions. He longed to help him see the light of Jesus.

One day that man finally said, "I don't want to hear another word from you. I'm sick of it." Before my friend could defend himself, the man continued, "I want you to understand. I know that you're right, that the beliefs that I claim to have are wrong. I know this is not the way to God, that the religion I belong to is a false religion, but what do you want me to do?

"My mom and dad were raised in this religion. My grandparents and my great-grandparents were raised in this religion. All my kids are raised in this religion, and so are all my grandkids. My entire family—my whole world—is wrapped up in this religion. If I renounce my faith, do you know what that's going to cost me? I would lose it all; my entire family would reject and disown me. I'd lose my entire social structure. I know the truth, but the price is too high."

This man deeply loves his family. I identify with that, and I am sure you do, too. But the problem is that his love for his family is greater than his love for God. It has become an idol. Idolatry is loving something else more than God, more than God's truth. Anything you love more than God is an idol.

Let me share Jesus' own words on this subject: "Whoever loves father or mother more than me is not worthy of me, and whoever loves son or daughter more than me is not worthy of me" (Matthew 10:37). You might say that's a heavy burden to bear. Then Jesus continued, "And whoever does not take up his cross and follow me is not worthy of me" (Matthew 10:38).

The single most important relationship in your life must be God. It must absolutely be God. Your greatest love and affection must be His, without exception. This is a great point to stop, underline, circle, and think about.

Your most important relationship in your entire life must be God!

This is the order of priority for your life: God first, above all else, followed by your spouse if you're married and then by any children you may have. Then comes your immediate family, such as your parents and siblings, your church family, your friends, and then everyone else in your life. There should be no one you love more than Christ, no one. He is to be your supreme treasure.

I live happily in the knowledge that my wife loves me very deeply. She's devoted to me, but her first love is Jesus, as it should be. She knows she is my best friend, my greatest human relationship here on earth, but my greatest love is Jesus Christ. The worst thing I could do for her, for my family, for everyone around me, is to make an idol out of my wife and love her more than I love God.

In fact, I can't love her the way I need to love her unless I love God first in my life and in my heart. There's something about the love of God that penetrates your heart and gives you the ability to love people more deeply than you can possibly imagine.

Media Idols

Let's discuss entertainment and technology. How much time do you spend watching TV or playing video games? For how long do you stare at that little screen that you carry around with you everywhere you go? I say that as someone who carries a little screen around with me everywhere I go!

Now compare that amount of time to the time you

spend with God. How does it compare to the time you spend reading the Word, being in prayer, meditating on and thinking about God, worshipping Him? What's the first thing you look at when you wake up? Is it your Facebook feed, or is it the Bible? What's the last thing you think about before you sleep? Is it what you read on social media, or is it how good God has been to you that day?

I'm not trying to give you a set of rules to live by. If that's what you take away from this book, then I've failed. Rather than legalistic rules, I want to provide litmus tests for you to examine your own heart.

Do you love God more than technology? How do you know? Do you worship the Lord, or do you worship endlessly at the altar of entertainment? There are endless options competing for your heart in entertainment, technology, hobbies, and interests you'd like to explore. It's easy to drift away from God.

You've seen it happen before. People get into a new hobby or a new interest and their life then begins to revolve around it. They hang around a new group of people and drop out of church. The next thing you know, they have traded gold for a sack of rocks.

There are many other things that can distract us from God, but you get the point. Anything you love or desire more than God can become an idol in your life. Anything you become obsessive about can become an idol.

Sports, career, stature in the community, your children or grandchildren, even your service to the church can be something you value more than you value your relationship with God. Pastors must guard themselves against this all the time. They can fall in love with being a pastor and lose their passion for the Lord who called them.

But it doesn't have to be this way.

The Greatest Commandment

And one of the scribes came up and heard them disputing with one another, and seeing that he answered them well, asked him, "Which commandment is the most important of all?" Jesus answered, "The most important is, 'Hear, O Israel: The Lord our God, the Lord is one. And you shall love the Lord your God with all your heart and with all your soul and with all your mind and with all your strength.' The second is this: 'You shall love your neighbor as yourself.' There is no other commandment greater than these."

—Mark 12:28–31

How can you please God? You are to love Him with everything that you are. Make Him the focus of your heart, the center of your identity. If you orient your life around this relationship, the rest of your life will fall in place as an expression of that love.

When God is the center of your life, you become a better parent, a better spouse, and a better sibling. It impacts your role as employee, employer, student, community member, neighbor, or friend. It defines how you treat other people—especially strangers—and even how you act when you're driving and someone cuts you off.

Every facet of your life should be influenced by your love for Christ. This love should flow through you not just at church, but also at home, at school, at work, in the doctor's office, at the grocery store, at the B&B when you're on vacation, or even when you're talking to that collection agent on the phone, because He is supposed to be the supreme love of your life.

What does that look like? How do you get there? Pretty simple. Loving Jesus is about obedience. Jesus said to His disciples, "If you love me, you will keep my commandments" (John 14:15). Jesus was making a direct correlation between our love for God and our obedience to His Word.

If you truly love Him—if your heart is indeed set on Him, if He's the center of your life, the supreme affection of your heart, and your greatest joy—then you will naturally become obedient. Obedience will be a by-product of your love for Christ, a consequence of that. Obedience is the natural outworking of our love for Jesus. But even more than that, He has given us the Holy Spirit to help us to be obedient.

> *And I will ask the Father, and he will give you another Helper, to be with you forever, even the Spirit of truth, whom the world cannot receive, because it neither sees him nor knows him. You know him, for he dwells with you and will be in you.*
> **—John 14:16–17**

No one is going to be perfect this side of heaven, but if God is your supreme love, it will be evident in your obedience. People who love God naturally begin to obey Him.

If you love Christ, then you'll also serve Him. It will just happen. You will want to serve Him by caring for people and ministering to them. Loving God is also about loving others. If you love God, you'll begin to love what

God loves, and He loves other people. Not just some, but *all* other people.

Jesus said the second greatest commandment is to love your neighbor as yourself. Why? Because God loves your neighbor. And understand your neighbor isn't just the person who lives on either side of you on the street, but everyone you come into contact with.

In the story of the Good Samaritan (Luke 10:25–37), a lawyer asked Jesus, "Who is my neighbor?" Jesus responded with this account:

> *Jesus replied, "A man was going down from Jerusalem to Jericho, and he fell among robbers, who stripped him and beat him and departed, leaving him half dead. Now by chance a priest was going down that road, and when he saw him he passed by on the other side. So likewise a Levite, when he came to the place and saw him, passed by on the other side. But a Samaritan, as he journeyed, came to where he was, and when he saw him, he had compassion. He went to him and bound up his wounds, pouring on oil and wine. Then he set him on his own animal and brought him to an inn and took care of him. And the next day he took out two denarii and gave them to the innkeeper, saying, 'Take care of him, and whatever more you spend, I will repay you when I come back.' Which of these three, do you think, proved to be a neighbor to the man who fell among the robbers?" He said, "The one who showed him mercy." And Jesus said to him, "You go, and do likewise."*
> **—Luke 10:30–37**

This parable illuminates the definition of the word *neighbor*, both in the word used in the original Greek and in the narrative context of its use. The Greek word for *neighbor* is *plēsion*, which means "any other man irrespective of nation or religion with whom we live or whom we chance to meet."[14]

That includes the people you really don't like that much, those you struggle to love, even those you say you hate. Jesus expands the definition of whom you're supposed to love to every possible human being, including your enemies.

> You have heard that it was said, "You shall love your neighbor and hate your enemy." But I say to you, Love your enemies and pray for those who persecute you, so that you may be sons of your Father who is in heaven.
> —*Matthew 5:43–45*

Your ability to love other people, including your enemies, is directly related to how much you love God. That means you cannot say you love God supremely in your life if you hate someone. If you harbor hate in your heart for someone in your life, God is not the One you're loving more than anything else. Something else has taken that place and you've become distracted at some level.

How do you fix this? How do you learn to walk in love with God? It's a process of growing in your relationship with God. It's about growing to know Him better. Like all relationships, it requires time and investment.

Keep your love for God first, and you'll find your distractions aren't nearly so appealing. Then your relationship with Him will grow and deepen for your good and for His glory. As the song goes, "Turn your eyes upon Jesus, look full in his wonderful face, and the things of earth will grow strangely dim, in the light of his glory and grace."[15]

Chapter Six Questions

Question: Are there any idols that almost kept you from becoming a follower of Jesus? How did your attitude toward these things change once you were saved?

Question: What material idols do you find the most tempting? What are some material possessions and lifestyle expectations that are an accepted part of your socioeconomic status? Have you ever stopped to pray and evaluate if these things are part of God's plan for you, rather than a societal and personal expectation of what you should possess?

_____

_____

_____

_____

_____

_____

_____

_____

_____

_____

_____

Question: Parenting can reveal many idols of the heart. Do you idolize your children's approval and acceptance so much that you cannot correct them? Would you give your child freedom and encouragement to follow God to the foreign mission field, to the inner city, or to a different educational or career path than the one you envision? What about a "prodigal" child? Are you willing for God to bring pain and sorrow into your children's lives to draw them back to Him? Evaluate idols that may be affecting your parenting.

Journal: As I mentioned in the very first chapter, if you want to make God the supreme love of your life, you must be in a position to hear Him in His Word. Do you have any idols in your life distracting you from your love of God? If so, what are they? Write them down and ask God to forgive you and help you to change.

Action: With what forms of technology/media are you most connected? Chart how much time you spend on each. In chapter one, you were encouraged to commit to a week-long technology fast. Identify the emotional impact that withdrawing from technology has had on you. Have you missed social media or video games more than you have missed or felt a loss from a skipped devotional time? What forms of social media or technology will you eliminate or significantly reduce in your life?

Chapter Six Notes

_____

_____

_____

_____

_____

_____

_____

_____

_____

_____

_____

_____

_____

_____

_____

_____

_____

_____

_____

CONCLUSION

An Awesome Adventure

I recently saw an image of a man sitting on the bow of a boat in the ocean while a great whale surfaced alongside the vessel. The man, however, was mesmerized by the phone in his hand and missed the amazing moment altogether. If we are not vigilant, our distractions will also cause us to miss out. We can be distracted by our phones, fears, misguided thinking, and idols and miss the huge, amazing adventure God has invited us into—the adventure of seeing, knowing, following, and serving Him. Our distractions make us lose sight of our great God and His great gospel. They cause us to try to live life on our own strength. They separate us from the Father and the life He wishes for us.

The only way to defeat the power of distractions is to put your attention fully onto Jesus. When your mind, heart, and eyes are focused on Him:

- He calms your fears and anxieties (Philippians

4:6–7).

- He renews your mind so it is conformed to His (Romans 12:2).

- He guides you—in how to think, how and when and what to speak, and how to behave (John 14:15–26).

You live in a world where single-minded focus on just about anything is a challenge. Everybody everywhere is multi-tasking, juggling, and spinning multiple plates at once. Because frantic busyness is so pervasive in our culture, it's exceedingly difficult to step off the hamster wheel and focus, truly focus, on Jesus. You also have the added challenge of the spiritual dimension: Satan himself works to contribute to your distraction.

However, single-minded focus on Jesus is the key to living the life you're meant to live. You must prioritize your time with Him and His Word above every other priority. This means:

- Spend time with God every single day through worship and prayer.

- Spend time in God's Word—reading it, studying it, and meditating on it—every single day.

- Do what God says through His Word.

I know I might sound like a broken record with these prescriptions, but I promise you they are the key, and I promise you they work. If you truly desire to know God intimately and to follow Him, this is how you do it.

I also know it's an uphill battle. Believe me, I fight it, too. Being a pastor doesn't make me immune to the challenge. But pursuing a healthy relationship with God is worth the effort. The time you spend with God and in His Word is never wasted. The Lord encourages, strengthens, directs, and blesses all your time with Him. It's what you were made for.

And as you walk with Him, grow in Him, and serve Him, you will live life to its fullest and bring glory to our great and glorious God and enjoy him forever.

About the Author

Sherman Burkhead is the senior pastor at First Baptist Church of Boron, California—a loving fellowship of growing disciples who want to go deeper in their faith and go broader in their outreach. As a former atheist saved by the grace of God later in life, Pastor Sherman is passionate about sharing the hope of the gospel of Christ with his community and beyond. And he is devoted to helping those who know Jesus mature in their faith and bare the fruit of salvation in their lives.

Pastor Sherman holds a degree in religion (Biblical and Theological Studies) and church ministry from Liberty University, and he is currently pursuing his Master of Divinity at Covenant Baptist Theological Seminary. He is husband to Kimberly, who serves alongside him as the children's director at First Baptist Church of Boron, and he is also a father of five and a grandfather of two.

REFERENCES

Notes

[1] Wesley, John. *Wesley's Revision of the Shorter Catechism.* Geo. A Morton, 1906, p. 1.

[2] Washer, Paul. "Busyness and Spiritual Discipline." Sermon. November 17, 2009. Heartcry for Revival Conference 2009. Heartcry Missionary Society. In SermonAudio. https://www.sermonaudio.com/sermoninfo.asp?SID=111709133810 1.

[3] MacArthur, John. *Our Sufficiency in Christ.* Crossway, 1998.

[4] Pascal, Blaise. *Pensées.* Dover Publications, 2003, p. 113.

[5] Aufenkamp, Nick. "A Simple Way to Pray Every Day." Desiringgod.org. February 6, 2017. https://www.desiringgod.org/articles/a-simple-way-to-pray-every-day.

[6] "Anxiety and Physical Illness." Harvard Health Publishing. Harvard Medical School. May 9, 2018. https://www.health.harvard.edu/staying-healthy/anxiety_and_physical_illness.

[7] Keller, Timothy and Kathy Keller. *The Meaning of Marriage: Facing the Complexities of Commitment with the Wisdom of God.* Penguin Books, 2013.

[8] Wiersbe, Warren. *On Being a Leader for God.* Baker, 2011.

[9] Piper, John. "What Do You Think About Contemplative Prayer?" Desiringgod.org. May 22, 2010. https://www.desiringgod.org/interviews/what-do-you-think-about-contemplative-prayer.

[10] Martin, D. D. "Christian Mysticism." In Daniel J. Treier and Walter Elwell, eds., *Evangelical Dictionary of Theology*, Baker, 1984.

[11] Hillerbrand, Hans J. "Martin Luther: German Religious Leader." Encyclopaedia Britannica. February 14, 2019. https://www.britannica.com/biography/Martin-Luther.

[12] "Idolatry." Merriam-Webster. https://www.merriam-webster.com/dictionary/idolatry.

[13] Origen. Quoted in Philip Graham Ryken, *Jeremiah and Lamentations (ESV Edition): From Sorrow to Hope.* Crossway, 2016, p. 185.

[14] Strong, James. "G4139 – plēsion." In *Strong's Exhaustive Concordance of the Bible*, Hunt & Eaton, 1894, quoted in Blue Letter Bible. https://www.blueletterbible.org/lang/lexicon/lexicon.cfm?Strongs=G4139&t=KJV.

[15] Lemmel, Helen L. "Turn Your Eyes Upon Jesus." CCLI Song # 15960.